THE GERMAN SHEPHERD

&

HONEY BUNCH

BY

GORDON & RAMONA HOFER

ISBN: 978-0-692-40084-5

Cover Design & Editing by: Valerie Nystrom Paine www.ValsyDesigns.com

I would like to thank my brothers and sister,

Glenn, Jerry and Marlette,

for being so supportive of our ministry.

INTRODUCTION

This book has been written in the hope that people in ministry will be encouraged and discover that every trial that comes our way has to be approved of by God. In the midst of trials, remember it is not about God, it's about you…and how you are going to respond. Are you going to get angry at God and the people who are mistreating you or are you going to get sweeter? Bitter or better? The decision is yours.

Tests and trials are the tools God uses to promote and refine you.

> *"He will sit like a refiner of silver, burning away the dross. He will purify the Levites, refining them like gold and silver, so that they may once again offer acceptable sacrifices to the LORD." Malachi 3:3 NLT*

One time when I was going through a test, I was praying and heard a loud alarm like you hear on the radio. "This is a test. This is only a test." Immediately God spoke to me that this was a test and nothing more. He said, "I am not mad at you. I just have to test you so I can promote you."

That word changed my life forever!

GORDON'S STORY

On April 11, 1949, the Lord brought me into this world. I was born into a German family on a little farm in South Dakota. It was a bittersweet day for my parents. God gave a son to replace one they had lost. My older brother, also named Gordon, died when he was only five years old, so when I came along they just named me Gordon too.

I was born with a club foot. My foot was turned inward and looked like a club. Without treatment, people who have a club foot appear to be walking on their ankles or on the sides of their feet. My parents took me to Sioux Falls, South Dakota to Dr. Mark Vandermark, a surgeon who operated on my right foot. Our family did not have a trustworthy car so friends and relatives would drive us back and forth to the hospital for check-ups. One time we rode the bus, I recall that the seats were covered in red velvet.

After my first surgery, the doctor told my mom to keep an eye on my foot in case it turned crooked again. It did so it was back to the operating table. I was in grade school at the time and I had never been very far from home or my parents. While they got me ready for the operation, I had to stay in a room without my mom. I was so afraid that she would not come back. She had a watch that she only wore on Sundays and special occasions so I requested that she put that watch on my wrist. I knew she would come back for the watch.

My mom and our church friends back home prayed that the Lord would touch me. The doctor said the procedure would be very painful but I experienced no pain at all. The little boy who shared the room with me did have pain from his operation. I remember him crying in agony. I also remember my mom prayed for him and the pain left right away.

It was hard going to school on crutches. The kids teased me mercilessly saying, "Here comes the cripple!" I played softball while on crutches. I would either strike out or hit a home run. It was a fight to survive.

One day a neighbor boy and I were throwing rocks into the stock pond. Stock ponds are built for watering livestock, irrigation, and fishing. The pond was six or seven feet deep. I slipped and fell in. I did not know how to swim. The neighbor boy ran and got my dad who jumped in and saved my life. He saw where the bubbles were, grabbed me, and threw me through the air like a football. When I landed on the shore with a thump, the impact brought me back to life. That was my first experience with CPR.

When you live on a farm, you learn to work hard. There are many farm accidents and it is common to see farmers with missing fingers and arms because of an accident. By the age of ten I was driving tractors and waking up early to do farm work. I fell off the tractor and got run over by a trailer. My face got very scratched up but nothing serious. Since we lived out in the country, I went to a one-room schoolhouse with ten other kids and one teacher. There were no indoor bathrooms and we had to bring our own food for lunch.

CHAPTER 2

RAMONA'S STORY

At the same time and in another place, my life began. I was born in a house in the suburbs of Virginia. I grew up with a love of horses and the Western way of life. At the age of 5 or 6, I remember climbing on the back of Mother's couch, anxiously waiting for the next exciting episode of Roy Rogers, King of the Cowboys, my hero! I sat with my eyes fixed to our little oval-shaped black and white TV.

I would always choose to be the horse when my friends played "house". I could gallop like the wind on all fours. On May Day, the only thing I wanted to dress up as was a cowgirl. After school each day I would run home to my small suburban backyard to see if what my heart so desperately longed for was there - a pony. It never was. With tears slowly sliding down my face, I would come back to reality.

We moved from Virginia to Florida the year I turned nine. I never stopped dreaming. At the age of twelve, I had to put my farm set aside. All my young life I dreamed of having a farm or ranch and would build my ranch in the Florida sand, making fencing out of sticks and thread. As I came into my teenage years, I had to stop playing horse, dressing up like a cowgirl and making ranches in the sand but I didn't give up my dream. How could a girl living so far from the West become a cowgirl? God knew.

My bedroom window faced the northwest. I would lie on my bed and welcome the summer night breezes through my open window and pray, "God, I want to marry someone from there," pointing toward the western night sky. God had a plan.

GORDON'S STORY

My walk with God started when I was ten years old. My mom took me to a Mennonite church in Huron, South Dakota where Evangelist Schmitt was preaching. He gave an altar call to accept Jesus but I was scared. My heart seemed to be pounding out of my chest but I did not go forward that night to receive Jesus. The next day Mom and I were making homemade ice cream with a hand-crank ice cream maker. I said to my mom, "Last night my heart was pounding hard while they sang 'Just As I Am.'"

> *Just as I am, without one plea,*
> *but that thy blood was shed for me,*
> *and that thou bidst me come to thee,*
> *O Lamb of God, I come, I come.*
>
> *Just as I am, and waiting not*
> *to rid my soul of one dark blot,*
> *to thee whose blood can cleanse each spot,*
> *O Lamb of God, I come, I come.*

My mom said, "Gordon, God is calling you. It's time for you to surrender to Jesus." She led me to Jesus Christ right there. She told me, "We are going back to church next Sunday night and you are going to make a public confession of your faith in Jesus." So that following Sunday night, off we went in our green 1954 Chevy. Mom told me, "When he gets done preaching, he will call for people to go forward; that's your cue to go up."

She put some oil on my face and dressed me in a nice little suit. They sang the song, and I got up to profess Jesus but something happened that I did not expect. Not only did I profess my Christianity but I also received the call to preach!

I had said to the Lord, "I will be a good Christian boy, but NOT a preacher." All the preachers I knew were sad and never smiled. So from the age of ten to sixteen I lived a decent life. My mom always made sure that we were in Sunday School and church each week, Wednesday night services and Vacation Bible School in the summer. My mom consistently read the Bible and prayed before breakfast every day.

One year, it rained so much that we could not do much farm work. I attended Vacation Bible School daily for three weeks straight. It was a nice break from farm work.

I had said I did not want to be a preacher but I started preaching to the cows as I milked them. I would sing "Just As I Am" as they walked into the barn to get milked.

Just as I am, thou wilt receive,
wilt welcome, pardon, cleanse, relieve;
because thy promise I believe,
O Lamb of God, I come, I come.

Just as I am, thy love unknown
hath broken every barrier down;
now, to be thine, yea thine alone,
O Lamb of God, I come, I come.

At each milking I taught them the various sermons that I had heard in church. They got saved and put their offering of milk in the bucket. I would also preach for hours as I drove along in our John Deere tractor.

GORDON'S STORY

I graduated from my small country school and went to a high school of fifty kids. "Wow," I thought, "all these new people that I can talk to." I got my first high school report card; there was one D- and the rest of my grades were F's. What was my dad going to say?

He said, "No problem. You can stay home and milk cows the rest of your life for me."

I went to my teachers and said, "We have got to get these grades up." So, by a miracle, I graduated from high school.

My dad said to me, "There are drugs are in our community and if you do drugs, I will kill you."

One day in the hallway of my high school a kid said, "Hey, Hofer, you want to do drugs?"

I yelled out loudly, "No, I do not want any drugs!" No one else asked me again.

My dad told me, "If you get a girl pregnant before marriage, I will kill you." Well, I was dating this girl who was not a Christian. She wanted to have sex with me but I remembered my dad's stern warning and I would not do it. That night, she broke up with me, leaving me upset and angry at God and at girls. For the next three years, I dealt with this anger by drinking, fighting, stealing, and cussing.

The devil can recognize the anointing on a person's life and will try to stop it.

My dear mother continued to pray for me. In fact she gave my name to every preacher she knew. She sent my name to Rev. Jack Glass, who was pastoring in Aberdeen, South Dakota. He took my name to the church choir who was practicing and they stopped and prayed for me. Several years later, when I was preaching in that same church, a lady came up to me and said, "I was there when the choir prayed for you."

During my senior year in high school, I landed a job at J.C. Penney. The store manager, Mr. Wolf, took a liking to me and taught me how to sell clothes. One day a preacher, Rev. Howard Cummings, came into the store and invited me to church. I said, "My mom must have sent you."

He said, "Yes." I told him I would go but I didn't. He and his associate pastor kept coming back until I decided that I would go once and then I tell him I hated him and his church. Surely he would never invite me again.

During my time away from God, I was secretly listening to a preacher on the radio who was from Jamestown, North Dakota. They would sing all the songs that I knew as a boy and on my way to school, I would cry like a baby while listening to that old preacher. God was softening my heart during the time I was a freshman in Huron College.

I finally went to church on a Sunday night and Rev. Cummings was preaching on hell and all who were going there. During his sermon, he named all the sins I had committed on Saturday night. I looked around the audience because people knew me in that church. I thought for sure that somebody had handed him a note telling him what to preach because Hofer was here. He continued to preach and I got upset with this guy. At the end of his message he said, "God loves you and has a plan for your life." When he said that, it was like an arrow left that pulpit, hit my hard heart, and broke it. Then they sang that song that was sung when I went forward as a ten year old, "Just As I Am".

Just as I am, though tossed about
with many a conflict, many a doubt,
fightings and fears within, without,
O Lamb of God, I come, I come.

Just as I am, poor, wretched, blind;
sight, riches, healing of the mind,

yea, all I need in thee to find,
O Lamb of God, I come, I come.

My heart began beating fast again. I said, "Jesus, do You still want me after all this sin?"

His answer was, "Yes!" Down to the altar I went, crying. My way back to God meant never going back to my old ways.

I called my mom immediately and said, "I am happy, so happy. Jesus is in my heart. You will never receive a call from the police again. It's over!"

The next day at work my boss said, "Your face is shining! What happened?" He named some fleshly things he thought I might have done over the weekend.

I said, "No! Last night I got saved! I am a Christian, and I will never do sinful things with you again."

He laughed and said, "It won't last. You are not a religious person."

I said, "You're right! I'm in a relationship with Jesus Christ!" This conversion was in the month of November and for five years I would call him and tell him that it was still working. My father also made a full commitment to Jesus three months after my coming back to God.

One week after coming back to Jesus, I attended the Sunday night service. I saw people around the altar with their hands raised, speaking oddly. I asked the pastor, "What are they doing?"

He said, "Speaking in tongues like in the book of Acts."

"What for?" I asked.

He answered, "Well, it gives you more power to serve Jesus."

I said, "I want that!" Fifteen minutes later, I was speaking in tongues and I have spoken in tongues every day since 1968.

GORDON'S STORY

Now that my life was on track again, I decided I needed a girlfriend. The mothers at our local church were not too excited about me dating any of their daughters. I remembered the pastor had preached about how Jesus had turned the water into wine, so I looked at my pillow and said, "You will turn into a pretty wife." I did that every night for one year!

There was a group of students from my college who were also attending the church. They took me under their wing and kept me involved with the group, going to different places to share Jesus. They asked me to come and share my testimony and I started to preach. Gaylon VanZee was one of the leaders that helped disciple me in those early months of my Christian life and he became a lifelong friend. He would always yell across our secular campus, "Hofer, have you made Jesus Christ the Lord of your life?" which was rather embarrassing.

After the first time, I would look to see if Gaylon was anywhere near before I walked across the campus. I would think, "Ok, coast is clear."

Then, suddenly, he would see me and yell, "Hey, Hofer, have you made Jesus the Lord of your life?" On a Sunday night in April, after my November conversion, I made Jesus the Lord of my life not just my Savior, and he finally stopped yelling at me.

My pastor was big on missions and he told me about a mission's outreach I should go on for one month in July. I was enrolled in a secular college at the time of my conversion but had a desire to go to Bible School. My pastor advised me to finish the year out at my secular college and then go to Bible school the next fall. The school I enrolled in was in Jameston, North Dakota.

So I signed up for the mission's trip, which was called Ambassadors in Missions. The cost was $400.00. It was a huge amount for me to raise back then. They told me I was accepted but I did not know what country.

I said to the Lord, "You know where I am going; please tell me." I heard a name that sounded like "Jamaica." I had never heard of it and thought maybe I had just made something up. So I went to the library and asked the librarian "Is there a country by name of Jamaica?" She said yes, and I almost fainted. I told everybody, "I'm going to Jamaica to preach," and sure enough, when the missions director announced where people were placed, he said, "Gordon

Hofer: Jamaica." I jumped up, shouting and praising God. That was the first time I had ever heard God speak so directly.

I got a job laying irrigation lines to earn enough money to go. We met in Miami, Florida for orientation. Young people got up and testified how God had just given them the money to go on the trip. I thought to myself, "What am I missing here? I had to work for mine." This was the beginning of my faith walk in the area of believing God for money to do His work. The trip was life changing and I preached In Jamaica. When I came home, I headed for Bible school in Jamestown, North Dakota.

I had my pillow and was praying daily for it to turn into a pretty wife. Pastors began asking me to come and preach and show the slides of my trip. It was an open door to start my ministry. Every weekend, I would go out and preach. During this time, God was beginning to take the rough edges off of me. I was a Christian but I was still struggling with sins of the past. Peter Walker was one of the Bible school teachers who operated in a deliverance ministry and the Word of Knowledge. A Word of Knowledge is an impression or knowing that gives you supernatural insight or understanding of circumstances, situations or problems. I sat in chapel and for the first time saw this gift in operation through Brother Walker. That night in prayer, I asked the Lord to tell Brother Walker what my problem was and, sure enough, the very next day he revealed it. I went to the altar and got set free. Praise God!

CHAPTER 6

RAMONA'S STORY

In 1965, I left my home in Florida and went to Philadelphia to live with my sister. While living there, I met and fell in love with a fine medical student and professional pianist. He romanced me for a whole year, taking me to concerts and horse shows and such. He had the ability to give me anything I wanted, including my ranch! We were to be married.

But by the Christmas of 1966, with a heavy heart, I realized my fiancé and I were not meant for one another so I said my last goodbye to him. God had other plans for us and our paths were to go in different directions.

During this time, my dearest friend and pastor's wife, Joyce Strader, received a letter from her mother, Grandma Wead, who lived in Vale, South Dakota. She asked Joyce if she knew a Christian woman who loved horses and the Western way of life because there was this certain Montana cowboy who was looking for a Christian wife. Did she ever know someone! Joyce knew just the woman - me!

To my amazement a few days later, I received a letter from Alzada, Montana. It was from a desperate, good-looking cowboy. He was determined not to live through another cold, lonely winter alone even if it meant simply corresponding with a woman who lived 1800 miles away. *After all, when you live thirty miles off the main road, a good Christian woman is hard to come by!* We became pen pals for over a year. *You know what? You can fall in love through a letter.* It was time to meet so he invited me to his ranch the fall of '68. Did I accept? You betcha! That was great news until I learned that he had another woman on the hook. *I had been playing second fiddle!*

They were in love but because she was a preacher's daughter and he was a cowboy, she wasn't sure if he was the one for her. When her dad found out about me, he walked into her room and made the announcement, "Your cowboy has found another." Immediately she picked up the phone and begged the cowboy to let her come out one more time before he made his final choice. He agreed so she made preparations to come immediately!

I was already on a three day bus trip when this drama took place. I was thirty miles from Rapid City, South Dakota when God spoke to me very plainly, saying, "Ramona, this is not to be."

With tears in my eyes, I said, "No, Lord, this can't be from you!" I tucked away what God had said and finished my long, weary trip to

Grandma Wead's home in Vale. I was to meet my cowboy at her church and then after the service, drive to his ranch in Montana.

The moment our eyes met I could hear it – a door slamming shut between us. What God had told me regarding this relationship must be true. I still went with him and tried to maintain a tiny bit of hope that our relationship could still work and that I hadn't already heard from God. After all, I was only 70 miles away from ranch life.

I stayed with him and his mother and dad for a week. I was in heaven - a ranch out west! I was so close to possessing my dream! But, as the week went on, I knew in my broken heart that it was not to be. The cowboy's true love had poured on all of her charms to win him back. As I rode alone on the prairie, I tearfully surrendered. "Lord, Your will be done."

With a broken heart, I went back to Vale for a few days to lick my wounds and decide what to do with my life. I did not want to go back to Florida. Meanwhile, Roy Wead, Grandma Wead's son, came to visit on his way to Trinity Bible College. He was accepting a new position as president of the school. When he learning of my dilemma, he asked me to come and be a student at TBI. I responded, "I haven't filled out an application and I have no money."

He said, "That's okay. You can fill it out when you get there."

Hooray! Another chance to find a cowboy! I told the Lord, "I'll go for only one reason, and that's to find a cowboy." That was okay with Him because He had a plan.

I spent one glorious year there, and, yes, I found two cowboys! Sadly the one I fell for didn't have eyes for me and I knew the one who fell for me wasn't the one. "Lord, won't this ever work out?" I asked.

When school got out, my sister invited me to come live with her in Texas. Jobs were scarce so things went from bad to worse for me financially. I was broke - so broke I thought there no way to ever recover.

One morning, while I was on my knees praying, I heard the Lord distinctly say to me, "Ramona, I want you to go back to school."

"But, Lord, I'm already two weeks late, and besides, I'm broke and have no way to get out of the mess I'm in."

He said, "Go back to school."

I responded, "If this really is You, Lord, have Joyce (my pastor's wife friend in Florida) call me."

That night, I got a call. It was Joyce! "Ramona, I want you to go back to TBC." She sent the money for me to fly back to Jamestown to begin a *very interesting* year at school.

CHAPTER 7

GORDON'S STORY

The buzz on campus was that Ramona Bunch was coming back to school. They called her Honey Bunch.

"What's that about? Who is this girl?" I thought.

Then, as I was walking into the college administration building, this girl came out and I heard an audible voice say, "This is your wife." I thought, "O my God, please make her beautiful in my eyes." She was but it took me several weeks to get the courage to ask her out on a date.

CHAPTER 8

RAMONA'S STORY

The first time I noticed Gordon was at church on a Sunday morning. He was singing in the choir. He was so skinny his Adam's apple bobbed up and down when he sang. But, he was a rather good looking guy…from a distance.

The first time I saw him up close was when I was coming out of the main door of the school. He was walking toward me. I noticed his big broad shoulders and handsome blue-black hair and the bluest eyes I had ever seen which looked at me rather strangely. Little did I know God had just spoken to him, "There goes your wife!"

I soon learned that he was a tough, gruff German that found it hard to express his affections. Full of hurts, he was in survival mode and would challenge anyone who crossed him. Growing up in a South Dakota German-Russian Mennonite home, the showing of affection or a physical embrace was non-existent. Being called by the town's kids a "dumb Russian" would put him into fight mode. Teachers would say he needed to go to Teen Challenge, not to TBC.

But I fell in love with this man. I saw in him, along with many other good things, that he loved God with all his heart and was sold out to Him. When he realized he was wrong, he was quick to repent and get it right.

The teachers started coming to me when they found out we were engaged. "Ramona, don't marry him. He'll do you wrong," they would say. "He has too many rough edges."

My answer to the teachers was, "I'm not marrying him for who he is now, but for who he will become in the future."

One night as I was praying, God said, "Ramona, are you willing to give him up?"

I thought, *Lord, are You saying I'm to give him up right now?*

"You will have to give him up in the future." I made a commitment to God that night and gave Gordon over to Him.

It took me two weeks to say "yes" when he popped the question because I didn't want to marry a preacher for several reasons. The first reason was that I grew up in a legalistic religious Pentecostal church that didn't treat pastors very well, and, besides, do you remember my dream? That was my second reason. In the end, though, I married this man from South Dakota.

GORDON'S STORY

Thank God she said yes because I was tired of praying for my pillow to become a wife. We dated for six months, and then married on May 3, 1970 in Lakeland, Florida. We had so little money for a wedding - it cost $70.00. My mom loaned me the money for my tux. A friend paid for the reception dinner. The office manager at the Ramada Inn in Lakeland said, "Your two nights in the honeymoon suite are free." He added, "I don't know who you are. My boss never gives anyone a free room!"

Then it was time to head back to Bible school. Ramona had graduated and I was a second year student. I got a job in Lakeland laying sod at $2.25 an hour – "green side up" they told me. We saved our money and I headed to my home town with my new bride. The whole trip back cost around $100.00, including 20 cents per gallon for gas; fortunately I knew some people we could stay with along the way. We spent the rest of the summer in Huron. I worked at a meat processing plant to earn enough money to get back to Bible school. We got a basement apartment and set up housekeeping.

One Wednesday, while heading to church, I told Ramona, "Do not get pregnant; we cannot afford children at this time."

After our pastor finished preaching, I went up to the altar to pray. I usually am loud but that night Ramona noticed I was very quiet. I had heard the voice of the Lord say, "Ramona is going to have a baby and the child shall be greatly used of the Lord."

So, on the way home, I said to Ramona, "You are going to have a baby. God says He will provide." I got a job at a cattle auction in Jamestown, and Ramona began to work for Bell Telephone as a bill collector. For sweet, soft Ramona, that was a stretch.

Ramona then announced to me, "Gordon, you are going to be a daddy." At that time I received an invitation to work at Teen Challenge. They offered me a salary of $25.00 a week plus room and food. So I asked my Bible school teachers if they thought I was ready and they released me to go.

Off we went to Ohio. By this time Ramona was already six months pregnant. The director was upset because Ramona was going to have a baby. Now she would not be worth much to them. He had wanted two people to work at the center for $25 a week. On July 30, our baby girl, Corrie, was born.

When I became a Christian, I immediately began to tithe and give offerings. God was teaching me to have faith that He would provide. I would go to the mailbox and money would be there. In just one day $75 came in. I was so excited I went to our staff meeting and shared what God had done. Nobody rejoiced with me so I did not share again.

God was providing in so many ways – even strange ways. While at Teen Challenge, a man named Charles asked me if I had a pillow he could use and I said yes. The next morning he asked if I would want to sell the pillow. I did not know what to say but then he said, "Will you take $50 for it?"

I said a very quick "yes"! He must have needed a wife too.

RAMONA HOFER'S STORY

Thus, our journey of faith and trust in God began. Our honeymoon consisted of a trip back to South Dakota. Since we only had money for gas, Gordon connected with two families as stopovers, one in northern Florida and one in the Smoky Mountains of North Carolina. Gordon miscalculated. We had to call Mom Hofer when we ran out of gas in Indiana. At that time, we didn't have faith to lay hands on that black Chevy and command her to be filled with gas. Mom was more convenient.

Arriving at his family's farm in Huron, South Dakota, Gordon introduced me as his new bride. They were shocked. "What! You are married?" they said.

Gordon responded, "Mom, Dad, I told you I was getting married. I even invited you to the wedding."

Mom Hofer was against it from the beginning because I was an "Englisher". I'd contaminate the German bloodline and Dad Hofer thought I was too skinny.

"You'll have to shake the sheets to find her! Besides, she's poor. You should have married the rich girl you met in school."

Two weeks after we arrived at the farm, Gordon left for a two-week mission trip to Germany. Three weeks after we married, he left me all alone! I recalled the Father's words: "Are you willing to give him up?" Now I understood.

As the years have gone by, God has given me the grace to be alone while he's on the road spreading the gospel.

Two years went by before I began to think Mom Hofer liked me...much less loved me. She told me what to do; she didn't ask. My job was to run the house, cook, clean, and continually pick up after them. At first, a little resentment tried to creep in because I wanted to be outside. I was finally on a farm - cows, sheep, pigs, turkeys, chickens, and ducks--the whole lot. I loved it!

One day after Mom ordered about 150 new baby chicks, I went out to the little pen they were kept in and crawled inside and sat with them. At first, they ran from me, but it wasn't long before they discovered my warmth and as I sat quietly, not moving an inch, they all snuggled next to me, in my hands, and climbed up on my legs. I was in heaven. Tranquility settled in with me and "my" chicks. About that time, Mom Hofer happened to walk by. She took one look, never said a word, shook her head, and walked on. To her, I was a weird Englisher.

I took pictures of everything that moved and of all the activities on the farm. *They laughed at me yet those pictures meant so much to everyone after Dad Hofer died.*

Dad thought of me as a city slicker - not much good on the farm. But one day, I proved him wrong. The baby pigs got out. Gordon's ten year old nephew was with us and Dad said, "Come on, boy. Let's get the pigs."

"Dad, can I go?" I asked. He looked at me curiously and said, "Ok, if you wanna."

Baby pigs were running everywhere and as one ran past me, I took a flying leap and caught him by his hind legs. I stood up with a big grin on my face as I held up the squealing piglet. Dad's eyes got as big as saucers and a huge roaring laugh came out of his mouth. City slicker, huh? Not anymore!

As time went on, God taught me to love Mom unconditionally, not to try to change her or oppose her ways. I grew to love her just as she was. Yes, there were trying days, but as the years passed, we grew very close. Mom Hofer, toward the end of her life, would call me often and our main topic was heaven. We would imagine the moment she'd see Dad Hofer and her beloved Savior. *God granted my desire to be by her side when she passed over.*

A short time after arriving in South Dakota, my first evangelistic road trip with Gordon was in the Black Hills and then we were to go on to Plentywood, Montana, for a weekend revival.

Being short on money, we had a little cook grill that we threw in the trunk, and Dad Hofer gave us two nice steaks--good old farm-raised beef. Noon came and we pulled over and had our first picnic lunch together then we drove on. As we came near the Black Hills, the car started shaking and finally slowed to a stop. Gordon and I sat there looking at each other for a while. Since we had no money, there was only one thing to do--pray. We laid hands on the car, called for the mechanic angels to come and commanded it to come to order. Gordon turned the key in the ignition and she started! We drove on to Rapid City for our first meeting.

Leaving Rapid City, we drove to Grandma Wead's in Vale, South Dakota. We stayed next door with Ray and Dorothy Dutton, my most beloved friends. It was Gordon's first time to meet them, and after lavishing generous hospitality on us, Ray handed Gordon a fifty-dollar bill. Gordon was completely taken aback and didn't know how to respond but finaly thanked him and we left for Montana.

Driving between Vale and Belle Fourche, we looked to our right and saw the South Dakota National Guard going through their maneuvers at Orman Dam. Excited to see them, I said, "Let's pull over and watch." As we slowed to a stop, we heard a hissing noise. A flat tire! *God knew it was coming and prompted Ray to give us the $50. It was just enough to get a new tire.*

We stopped at a friend's ranch in Montana on the way to Plentywood and spent the night there. She handed us a card congratulating us on our marriage. In it was $20, just enough gas money to get us to Plentywood, Montana, for our first revival meeting! *The Lord is our keeper. We will put our trust in him.*

We lived with Mom and Dad Hofer for two years. During that time, Gordon would leave and go on the road preaching. I would stay behind taking care of our precious little bundle, our first child Corrie. Four months before our second precious bundle was born, Dad Hofer passed on to Glory in January 1973. The next four months were very difficult for Gordon. Right after his dad died, he had to leave to meet ministry obligations. He spent three weeks in cold, snowy, lonely Norris, South Dakota on an Indian reservation. He had a very good meeting among the Native Americans but his heart was broken over his dad and he was lonely for me and Corrie.

GORDON'S STORY

One day while I was working at the Teen Challenge center, I received a phone call from a pastor who wanted to hire me as his youth minister. He offered me $200 a week plus a house. Well, that was a no-brainer; I accepted. We resigned our position at Teen Challenge and went to our new position. When I got there, he offered us only $20 a week and a home. This news was very hurtful but we went to work anyway and saw the youth group grow from twenty kids to one hundred in three months. At that point, I could not afford to stay there any longer. I had to feed my family. We packed up and went back home to South Dakota. We ended up in the farm house with my folks. I got a job working construction as a gofer – running errands or performing simple tasks. On Sundays, I would preach and then be back to work on Monday.

At this point, I began booking meetings in advance. One day I was at a friend's house and asked if I could use his phone to make a long distance call. I told him I would watch the minutes and pay him. There was a pastor in Piedmont, South Dakota that I needed to call about having a meeting. My friend said it would be cheaper to write but I knew God had said to call, so I called. The pastor answered and I introduced myself as Evangelist Hofer and asked if he would consider me coming to his church. He said, "We are having a leaders' meeting to discuss what evangelist we should invite! I guess God answered; when can you come?" God was providing.

I preached for an hour on Daniel in the fiery furnace and Shadrach, Meshach, and Abednego in the lion's den. What an embarrassing mistake, and poor Ramona had to sit through it and smile! My dad gave me a 1964 Chevy to travel in with Ramona and baby Corrie. We stayed in homes of pastors or church people. For the next five years, I was able to travel full time in South Dakota, North Dakota, Minnesota, Iowa and Montana. I would write to pastors two weeks ahead and ask if they could get a baby crib for Corrie. Not one pastor managed to get one and so at the age of two, Corrie had to sleep between Ramona and me. When we stayed in homes, people often would say, "Don't let her touch that," or "Oh no, she broke that."

That was enough for me, so I said to the Lord, "I want a motor home."

So I began to pray! One morning at the farmhouse, God spoke and said, "Today, go buy a motorhome."

I said to Ramona, "I'm going to town to buy a motorhome." I went to the dealership and told the owner what I wanted.

He said, "I have this 20-foot motorhome," and gave me a price. He then asked, "What do you do?"

"I am evangelist," I said.

He said, "I will sell it to you for what I have in it. Do you have a down payment?"

"Yes, that 1964 Chevy", pointing to my car in the parking lot. I went downtown to the bank, borrowed the rest of the money from one of my dad's old banker friends and went home with a new motorhome. It was small but we had our privacy. We traveled in South Dakota, North Dakota, Nebraska, Minnesota, and Wisconsin in that 20-foot motorhome. We loved it.

We paid $7,200 for the motorhome, drove it for one year, putting 12,000 miles on it, and sold it for $7,200. Then we bought a 35-foot 5th-wheel, which at that time, was one of the bigger ones. We felt so blessed to go from a 20-foot to 35-foot travel trailer. By now we had our second daughter so Corrie and Heidi had their own beds. They also had a puppy and a goldfish. Ramona made the trailer into a home on wheels. For five years we traveled in that trailer as God continued to open doors. Back then, if I received $200 for preaching Sunday through Thursday that was great.

CHAPTER 12

RAMONA'S STORY

After Heidi's birth, the Lord spoke to Gordon just as he was waking up one morning and said, "Go buy a motor home."

This was our first step of faith in action because we had very little money to live on let alone enough to buy a motor home. Gordon turned over in bed and said to me, "The Lord just told me to go buy a motor home." That wasn't a problem for me to accept because my whole life had been spent depending on God. I had stood on the doorstep of Trinity Bible College penniless and God worked it out for me to get in. As a matter of fact, I never thought about money. My Daddy God would supply. God had prepared me for Gordon.

I said, "Go!"

I was tired of sleeping in such uncomfortable places while we were on the road ministering. The various churches would usually only provide lodging in homes or churches where I would spend a sleepless night with my baby between me and that big German who could have easily rolled over and smothered her.

We had a car Dad Hofer gave Gordon, and with that as a trade-in, God miraculously opened a door for us to buy a 19-foot motor home.

Corrie, now two and a half, slept on the couch, and Heidi, only eleven days old, slept in her basinet on the front seat of the cab. We slept up over the cab in a 3/4 bed with six inches between us and the ceiling. We could hardly turn and I certainly wouldn't move because he took two thirds of the bed! We didn't care. We were happy. We were in our own "home" on the road. I remember Corrie and me bouncing along on the bed, laughing as Gordon drove happily along to our first meeting.

We lived one and a half years in that thing. Through cold winters and hot summers, but it was home. Later God rewarded us with a two-bedroom, 35-foot fifth-wheel. It had two doors and a bath tub. I thought I'd died and gone to heaven. It was home to the girls.

Life on the road was tough for us though we had some precious memories as a family. There was the tearing down and setting up of the motor home every time we moved. Washing our clothes in a different Laundromat each week but we had our own space and we were together.

CHAPTER 13

GORDON'S STORY

I was speaking at one church, and the pastor said, "Wow, more people are attending your meetings; you should get $600."

So I was all excited and thought, *Wow that will be wonderful.*

After the meeting was over, he handed me $150 and said, "You do not need more than this," and slammed the door in my face and left. I was so hurt and disappointed by his treatment that I cried for two hours while driving down the road. *Lesson learned—I was depending on man and not God to provide!*

Later in the 1970's, I was traveling and decided to stop at a big church convention. At the time, I was going through a very difficult time. I walked into the big church and stopped a well-known pastor and asked for prayer and he blew me off. He was too busy for me. That day I made a vow that when someone wanted me to pray, I would stop right then and pray with them. By God's grace, I did not want to treat others as I had been treated.

CHAPTER 14

RAMONA'S STORY

Gordon was a young preacher just out of Bible school and he believed that he was God's gift to the world. He was, but not in the way Gordon was thinking. He couldn't understand why the big time churches wouldn't have him. I knew but just kept quiet. It was not my place to show him. It was God's, in His time.

In trying to please pastors and to look good in their eyes, he made many demands of me. I had to be in church every night. Rarely did I get a break. My girls had to learn to be very quiet in the pew and not cause any distractions. I spent many nights in the nursery. It was a German custom that childcare was totally the woman's responsibility, so he'd leave early and I would have to get the girls and myself ready and walk with both girls on my hips to the church.

I am saying this because if you think marrying God's gift to you is going to be paradise, you've got another thing coming. They come with "some assembly required". This fact develops character in us.

God's gift to me through all of this was developing a merciful heart and patience as I waited to see what God would do to develop this awesome man of God.

Gordon decided to start singing at his meetings so he bought some musical accompaniment tapes. He has a beautiful voice but his timing with the taped music would often be off. The musical key? Well, that was often missing too. It was embarrassing. I wanted to slide under the pew but I sat there and smiled.

Here's a marital pointer for you: *Help your spouse develop good character and their God-given skills. Pray for and develop a merciful heart with great patience. The words you speak about and to your mate have power – for good or evil.*

CHAPTER 15

GORDON'S STORY

One of the challenges of being an evangelist is filling the calendar with meetings. Years ago I would write letters requesting preaching engagements and put together my calendar. I would then follow up with a phone call. Once, we ended up going to a camp meeting in Georgia. Only a few pastors knew me there. One afternoon, the District Superintendent was sweeping the tabernacle. I went up to him and said, "I think I can handle this broom; you go do something else."

That night, in front of 500 people, he said, "Today an evangelist took a broom away from me. Book this man for meetings!" I preached in Georgia for about one year.

CHAPTER 16

RAMONA'S STORY

Going on the road as an evangelist was a new step of faith for us. We never made demands as to what we should be paid (that has always been our policy to this day). We were truly a faith ministry. Coming from his background, this was tough for Gordon because he was trained to be the provider for the family. He felt he was solely responsible for provision for himself and his family. "You are the man! You make it happen." To completely rely on God was a new thing for him.

God never forsook us. He overshadowed us and cared for us everywhere we went, even though we wondered at times if we'd make it to the next place. I made our fifth-wheel home and we had many good memories.

GORDON'S STORY

I met a missionary to Chile. He wanted us to come and do tent meetings in Chile. We started raising money for the three-month stay. It was there, I believe, that God planted in my heart a love for Latin American people. Our daughters, Corrie and Heidi, went with us. I still remember them playing in the sand box with the kids in Chile. We flew down but decided to take a ship back to Panama and fly home from there. It was a wonderful experience spending twelve days on a freighter, seeing the different ports and going through the Panama Canal. My girls still talk about this trip.

One of the things we tried to do as we traveled was to have some fun days with the family. We wanted to make the ministry exciting and fun and to take time for them. I was very happy traveling as an evangelist. The Lord has given me a good memory in remembering people. When we traveled, people would come to Jesus. Then when I would go back to that church, I would ask for them by name or by their occupation. The pastors would say that they did not know where they were. I would ask, "Did you get their names or follow up with them?"

The answer over and over was, "No, we did not." That response really bothered me. It was at that point that God put a pastor's heart inside of me.

My messages changed from those of an evangelist to those of a pastor. At times, I would be walking around outside at 3 AM crying out to God for change. Then I got a call to pastor a church in Spearfish, South Dakota. At the time they had twenty people and were meeting in the basement of a Masonic Temple. I was filled with excitement for the new assignment of finding property and building a church. My ministry changed from evangelism to pastoring. What an adjustment! As a pastor, I had to learn to make decisions with a board of a church.

The church grew and soon we moved the church to a local college. We met in a building that had three flights of stairs. Each Sunday we hauled song books and instruments up all of those steps. We grew to 200 people in that building. An amazing feat since he town itself was only around 5,000 people at that time.

I remember the day I went to a real estate office to look for land. The realtor took me to a piece of land beside an old slaughter house and said that would be a good place for a church. It upset me that he thought that was a good place. I said to the Lord, "I will knock on doors to find land; I do not need a real estate agent."

For six months I combed the city looking for land. Finally, I met a man named Walt. I asked him if he would sell his land but he said no. However, we really hit it off, and I met with him for coffee once a week as a friend. One day, he said, "Did you find land for your church?"

"Not yet," I said. Then, to my surprise, he told me he wanted to sell me the land. I was so excited. I offered to get the lawyer and draw up the papers.

"No," he said, "we do not need a lawyer. I said I want to sell the land to the church." Then he said, "Put out the palm of your hand and spit in it", which I did. He did the same and we shook hands. That is how I bought 29 acres of land for the church.

Two of our leaders and I went down to Springfield, Missouri, to put together the money to build the church. These men were talking about such a large amount of money that I was afraid. My plan was to call Ramona and tell her to pack up. We were going to get out of there. Then I read a sign in the office in Springfield that said, "Do something so big for God that only He can get the credit." That sign changed my life. We started building the church and met in a tent throughout the summer while the church building was going up. The tent was in terrible condition. Every Saturday some faithful ladies of the church would come and patch the holes in the tent.

We baptized people in horse tanks in the tent. During nearly every service, people would come to Jesus. I loved the city. We got into the new building and had the pastor that won me to Jesus come and speak at the dedication service; that was really special. In Bible school they taught us to only dance in the Spirit and to dance with eyes closed. One Sunday morning in church, I got happy and wanted to dance. So I closed my eyes and started dancing and fell off the platform. The piano player stood up while she played the piano to see if I was alright. I wrecked my watch and white shirt.

After the service, I said to Ramona, "I felt the Lord wanted me to dance."

She said, "There is nowhere in the Bible that says to dance with eyes closed; next time for everyone's safety, dance with eyes open."

As an evangelist I was at a church for 3-5 days which was no problem. But being a pastor was different; and I found out that not everybody likes the pastor. I never could figure out why people would come to church just to cause trouble. There was a wealthy older man that would always cause trouble in the church. One day we had a meeting and I was warned he was coming to cause trouble. The Lord gave me Matthew 18:18, *"I tell you the truth, whatever you bind on earth will be bound in heaven, and whatever you loose on earth will be loosed in heaven."*

In agreement we bound the spirits in that man. I said, "Lord, if he has something good to say, let him speak; if not, then silence him." For the whole two hours of the meeting, he said nothing. Even though we started out with those twenty people, we never acted like a little church; we acted like a big church. I was on two radio stations and had a TV program. My dream was to stay at that church forever. Then one day, as I was driving I read the sign that said "Spearfish— 20 miles" and I realized the excitement was gone. The Lord told me it was time to move on. My response was "Oh no, Lord, please" but the answer was the same.

There were some great people there that had helped me and tolerated me through my lessons of pastoring my first church. We resigned the church thinking that many calls would come to me because the Lord had blessed us. However, no one called for me to pastor; we were in the desert. We went to Lakeland, Florida for a while then came back to stay with my brother in Montana. I would candidate for churches but did not feel right about them. I desperately needed to find a church and get settled again.

RAMONA'S STORY

After the trials, tests and victories on the road, we took our first church in Spearfish, South Dakota in the later part of the 1970s. I was delighted to go back to the Black Hills of South Dakota but a little apprehensive about taking a pastorship. I felt severely inadequate to be a pastor's wife. You see, Gordon didn't marry a perfect wife. I also had baggage that I carried into the marriage which God would have to lift off of me in His time. *It would take many years for this to come about!*

Settling in, we were thrilled to be living in beautiful Spearfish, South Dakota. Frank Hoffmeyer, a deacon in the church who was to become a very close friend, offered to buy our fifth-wheel. Corrie, now five, watched tearfully as it drove away. It was the only home she knew. We were able to use that money for the down-payment on our first home.

We met with our little congregation of 17 for the first time in a rented room. After that, we started meeting in the basement of the Masonic temple. We had no idea of these people's beliefs but we knew God would meet with us wherever we met. The church began to grow very rapidly and in a short time, our congregation of 75 began to meet in a hall at Black Hills State College.

Gordon began to look for land and God miraculously provided 30 acres for our new church building. The next summer, the South Dakota church headquarters loaned us a tent which we put on the property to use for services while the building was going up. Every week, the ladies of the church would meet to patch up all of the new tears in our aging tent.

One Saturday, while Gordon and our two older daughters were down at the grounds helping to set up for a youth rally; I stayed home alone with Beth, our twelve-year-old and third daughter. A bad storm suddenly came up. I ran into Beth's room and grabbed my sleeping daughter and headed for the basement. We hunkered down under Gordon's big metal desk (his office was in the basement) and prayed. This kind of storm was nothing new to me. I had prayed and demanded tornadoes and hails storms to lift and go around us a number of times while living in our motorhomes. I watched out the window as the wind mowed down my beautiful snapdragons. The worst of it only lasted a few minutes so after it passed, I walked upstairs.

It had been a tornado and it had moved a house across the street off its foundation! The deck behind the neighbor's house had been thrown into our front yard - 15 feet from our house. The tornado had jumped over our house and set down again in a neighboring subdivision. *You learn to trust God in every situation.*

Soon it was time for Gordon and his church board members to meet with a contractor. For a 27-year old with no previous experience in building a large structure this was overwhelming. Gordon walked in the contractor's office in fear and trepidation. As the men were talking, he had the overwhelming desire to jump ship and head home, gather us up, and leave town. His eye fell upon a plaque on the desk: "Building something so big that only God gets the credit!" That did it. Peace came to his heart. "I can do that." Thus, our first church was built.

During this time, our fourth daughter, Michelle, was born two days after Christmas, 1979. She was a beautiful, bubbly baby. She became our "court jester". She kept me in laughter.

In Spearfish, we began to ask God for the ability to discern the motives of our brothers and sisters in Christ. Not all of them sought to do things God way. This was when Gordon learned to put anger behind him, forgive and let God work in the hearts of those who opposed him or the work God wanted to accomplish in the church.

No matter where you go, there are those who want to control and get the glory. One such person was a business man in town who began to come to church with his following. He held prayer meetings at his home every week. He was a pleasant sort of fellow and everyone liked him, including Gordon.

As time went on, Gordon came to me and said, "I think I'll ask him to be in leadership. I'm going to talk to him about being on the board."

Immediately, I had red lights flashing. I responded, "No, I don't think that's a wise decision right now. You don't know him well enough. I don't trust him."

This was a new experience for Gordon - his wife giving a negative opinion about his decision. We came to a compromise. He would pray for one week before making his final decision. A couple days later, while praying in His office, this man's face appeared to him. He had his normal kind-looking face. All of a sudden, horns grew out of his head and his demeanor changed into a sinister expression. Within a week, a deacon came to Gordon and told him that this man had been going behind his back speaking against him, trying to place doubt in the hearts of the people about his leadership. Gordon was grateful for my gift as a seer in the house of the Lord.

Here's a marital pointer for you: *In the book of Genesis, it talks about being a "helpmeet" to your spouse. That means as a couple, we are to walk together as one, encouraging and lifting one another up and watching each other's backs. Your mate can see your blind side.*

After five and a half years and successfully raising up a solid church of 200 people, Gordon felt his work was done there. Because he had been so successful, he felt God would immediately place him in a better position. He just knew churches would be calling him, "Come to us!" So he resigned before getting another position.

GORDON'S STORY

During the time with my brother Glenn, I got a job as a waiter in a restaurant to take care of my family. Before I became a waiter, I had never tipped. The Lord allowed me this lesson; I was a waiter for three weeks. At first, I was so depressed and upset, but then the Lord said, "I want you to work hard and become the best waiter you can be." This taught me to be a servant like never before and now I tip everyone whether they give me good service or bad service. God wants to teach you things through each situation. He is not being mean; He wants to teach you. If you do not learn the lesson, you will have to take the test over and over until you pass.

While I was at my brother's home in Montana, the sheriff pulled up to his house. He delivered a message to me that Frank, one of my former deacons, had been killed in an accident and his wife wanted me to come to do the funeral. By this time the church had a new pastor but because I knew Frank better, they asked me to come. I met with the new pastor who told me that after the funeral he wanted me to leave and never come back to the city again. I was shocked by his insensitivity. I had just lost a very good friend and he was treating me like a dog. Even though I am the German Shepherd, it's not fun being treated like one. However I performed the funeral and then did what the new pastor had requested. After the funeral, Frank's wife asked me to speak to his employees and walk around the business and counsel his coworkers which I did.

Afterwards the Lord instructed me to go on a three day fast to get directions. In those three days the Lord opened up a month of evangelistic meetings for me. During this month, I got connected with a church in Minnesota. They asked me to become their pastor.

The day I was to candidate at the church, the Lord spoke to me and said, "You will deal with the man on the third row to your right."

I thought, "Oh my God, what have I gotten myself into?"

We took the challenge. The church was old and when you opened the door, you smelled sewer gas. That was our first hint of what was ahead. Immediately, we ran into conflict with the elders in the church. The Lord said, "Check out the history of the church." In forty years it had twenty pastors. An older gentleman gave me the most problems and had to be removed from office. We also were transitioning the church from singing from song books to using an overhead projector. One would have thought I was the antichrist. The congregation had no respect for leadership at all! The sound man would not listen to me and was defiant; the place was very difficult.

We lived in the church parsonage. I was told that one of the leaders would go through the parsonage while the pastor was not at home. When I heard this, I changed the locks and made an announcement that anyone who came into the parsonage without my permission would be treated as a robber. Religious people in our churches would complain that my piano player was playing too loudly. So I went into town and got some foam rubber to put in the piano to soften the sound.

Several weeks later, we had a guest pianist who began to play and said, "This piano feels like it has foam rubber in it," and opened the piano in the middle of his concert, pulled out the foam rubber, threw it on the floor, and continued playing. Later I took the foam rubber to the dump. You can never make religious people happy; forget trying. The bad thing is that they are usually in leadership and have the money.

By this time the Lord had blessed us with four daughters – Corrie, Heidi, Michelle and Beth. When we were in this city the two older ones were teenagers and rebellion was thick. As I look back, I wish I would have handled things differently but it was a mess. In a little town news travels fast. Most of the people in the church were not supportive during my family's problems. One man came up to me and said, "If you cannot get your family in order, you need not be a pastor." He never encouraged me once in the five years I was there. The town's people were kinder to me than the church people whom I was pastoring. We also built a new church building at that place as well.

The church members would write letters to the district office smearing my name. It got so bad that the district superintendent came and asked me to sign a paper that allowed him to go throughout the city to ask people about me. He came back with a good report and knew that all the things that the church folks had said were false. I was vindicated, but the storm was still brewing. There were real witches in that city and they visited our church from time to time to cause me trouble. It was five years of warfare.

Ramona's Story

In our organization, there were no mentors for a young preacher struggling to find his way, no one to give him advice. Gordon only got letters of correction if he did anything wrong in their eyes or if someone had a complaint or accusation against him. He was called on the carpet regularly at the "ministers' retreat"- which was every year. We were never allowed to know who our accusers were. All of the accusations against us were false. Where are the fathers in the body of Christ? *We needed fathers who would take us younger, struggling ones under their wings and disciple them.* Gordon would not have made such a quick decision if he had had someone to guide him and give him good council.

But God used this time in our lives to change our attitudes and make us more like Jesus. Through the coming year, Gordon and I learned to trust Him for provision in every move we made. Leaving Spearfish, we decided to drive to Lakeland, Florida, to my home church. Frank had loaned Gordon his "banana boat", a big brown and yellow Ford station wagon. It was ideal for hauling our four children, two poodles, and all our stuff!

Somewhere in Nebraska, the gas pedal fell to the floor and the car rolled to a stop. We were in the boonies with very little money to spend on a broken-down car. This time we didn't look to Mom Hofer for help. Gordon got out of the car and lifted the hood.

The girls looked at each other. "What is Dad doing?"

Gordon wasn't a mechanic. I turned to the girls. "Let's pray!" I laid my hands on the dash and commanded it to come back to order in Jesus' name. I didn't know that at the same time Gordon was commanding the demons to get out! He slammed the hood and climbed back in the car. Low and behold, the gas pedal had come back up. We drove on to Florida. *God is good, all the time. Need a mechanic, God has lots of mechanic angels, no charge!*

We arrived up in Lakeland, Florida, extremely low on money. We could not find a dwelling we could afford. At last, broken, fearful, and standing in the vestibule of the church there in Lakeland, we looked at each other and said, "What shall we do? Where shall we go from here?"

In walked Christy Jordan, one of my dearest lifetime friends from South Eastern Bible College. "Gordon, Ramona, God spoke to me on the way home and said, 'Go get Gordon and Ramona. They are at the church. Take them home.'"

Humbling as it was, we were so relieved. If I had to stay with someone, there was no one I'd rather be with than Christy. I had spent many a hilarious time with her. She was the bubbliest, funniest friend I could ask for. She would always lift my spirit.

After two weeks with her and her beloved, long-suffering husband, Dave, a rental opened up across the street and we moved in there. I can hardly remember where all of the furniture came from but somehow we had enough beds to sleep in and a couple chairs to sit on.

Gordon was at a total loss as to what he was going to do or where he was going to go. Nothing was working out for us there. A sense of great insecurity moved upon him. I had never seen my husband in such a state of mind or emotion. But our God is faithful. It was during this time I began to notice a quiet rebellion rising up in Corrie our oldest daughter.

CHAPTER 21

GORDON'S STORY

Our oldest daughter was rebelling and causing problems in our home by running away, dating unsaved young men, drinking, and taking drugs. We had her put into a drug rehab facility. Our family was being attacked.

For some reason, Ramona and I went to a meeting, where a prophetic woman called us out and said to me, "You are like Phillip the evangelist who had four daughters," and she began to describe our family situation and how God was going to greatly use our daughter. We were so excited; this was the first word we had received from a prophet and so we thought my daughter would change right away. However she got worse.

Another prophetic individual spoke about how God was going to minister to our family. It gave us hope but again she got worse. Then the prophets taught us to do warfare with these words and go into intercession. During this time, we would bring these prophets into our church. The prophets would prophesy over our family and speak the future.

The old-time church people who did not understand would say, "Those prophets are false; look how terrible this preacher's kids are."

Prophets pull open the curtains and say, "This is what the Lord has for you."

I remember saying to the Lord that if He would put a prophetic mouth in me to bless people, I would receive it.

"But one who prophesies strengthens others, encourages them, and comforts them." 1 Corinthians 14:3 NLT

That began to happen and soon we were going to a lot of Christian International meetings. We brought many of their prophetic people to the church in Minnesota. Every one of them would say the same thing over our family—that God was going to use them. The fact that they were prophesying made the church people very upset.

One day God gave me a Word of Wisdom. When I came into the office, the Lord told me to tell the word to my secretary, a single mom. "You are not to go to the bars anymore because God is going to send your husband to your front door." She married the UPS man soon after that!

I began to prophesy more frequently and bring more prophetic people to the church. One prophet came to a service when the church was full but 90% of those there were visitors. The prophet told me, "Your days are numbered in this place." That was on a Thursday. On Friday, we had a board meeting and the board members asked me to resign, which I happily did.

Ramona's Story

After one month in the rental, Gordon got up and announced, "We are leaving!"

"When?" I asked.

"Tomorrow morning."

"Tomorrow morning?!"

"Yes! I don't want to pay another month's rent!"

"Where are we going?" I asked, bewildered.

"To my brother Glen's house in Redlodge, Montana."

I can surely say life has been adventurous and never boring with Gordon Hofer! I packed everything in twelve hours. Arriving in Redlodge, we began to settle in. Glen and Selby had a daughter a little older than Corrie. They gave us her room and all the girls slept on the living room floor. I got a job at the Bull and the Bear restaurant as a dishwasher and salad maker. I saw an opening as a waiter for Gordon and approached him about it. Being in a desperate, humbling situation, he went and applied for the job and was hired on the spot by a desperate employer. How low can a man of God go - having to put on an apron? He would wait on a table, then go into the men's room and cry.

Tearfully, he'd ask, "Lord, how can I do this?"

The Lord answered, "Go out and be the best waiter you can be!"

Before this, I'd get upset with Gordon. He'd never give a tip. That job cured him. Hallelujah! He's a generous tipper now.

During that time, Gordon went to Wisconsin to try out for a church there so we made arrangements for me to fly there to meet him. I had to fly into Denver first. I noticed they had placed me in the back of the plane so I went up to the desk and asked if there were any seats further ahead.

She looked at me and asked, "Where would you like to sit, in the bulkhead?"

Being new at flying, I didn't know what the bulkhead was. I thought she meant the very first row in economy. "That would be fine, thank you." I walked right through first class, looking for 3A. The first seat in economy was number 6. With trepidation, I walked back in first class and said to myself, "I don't belong here."

The Lord plainly answered, "Sit down; I put you here."

They placed a lace tablecloth on my tray and served me a delicious meal on real china. The Lord gave me a seat where I could look to the north on this autumn night. He put on a show for me, northern lights danced in the crystal-clear moonless night! I was overwhelmed. The presence of God came over me. "See, this is for you, my princess!" *During those days of feeling less than nothing, the Father assured me that, in His sight, I was his princess, betrothed to His Son. Glory to God!*

We tried out for pastorship in a seemingly comfortable situation. But as I walked in and sat and watched, my seer gift clicked in. It was a family-run church. Religious controlling spirits were embedded in it. Gordon asked me what I saw, and I relayed to him what the Lord showed me. He had a witness and so declined their offer. He had told the girls he wouldn't come back without a church home to bring them to. He had another church in Michigan that was interested in him.

It is amazing how the demonic information line can be so informed. While we were resting in our hotel room, Gordon got a call. It was the head deacon at the Michigan church. He was furious that Gordon would be looking elsewhere other than their beloved church to pastor. How did he know? He shut us down quickly. Gordon hung up ashamed. Once again, we had nowhere to go. It seemed God had put him on the shelf and abandoned him. He felt helpless, alone, and worthless - pretty low for being "God's gift to the world".

At that moment, I saw this man of God grow more humble and mature. He looked up and said, "God, I still love you!" We went back to Glen's feeling dejected and with Gordon feeling like a failure. The next morning, Gordon and I were awakened by a very sad phone call. Frank Hoffmeyer, his dearest friend and former deacon in Spearfish, was killed in an auto accident. Joanne, his widow, asked Gordon to come and officiate the funeral. We packed up, gave hugs to Glen and Selby and left for Belle Forenche, South Dakota, where Joan lived.

We had gone full circle. The funeral was held in our former church which Gordon built while in Spearfish. With a broken heart, Gordon buried his dearest friend. After the funeral, the newly-hired minister called Gordon in the office and said, "I never want you to walk through these doors again! You're not liked or welcomed here." How much more stripping can the man of God endure? While we were pastoring there, a coup had risen up against us, and some disgruntled people wanted us out. We forgave and worked through it - learning to lean on God.

We left when the Holy Spirit said, "Go." Evidently the "Gordon haters" gathered around this pastor and filled his ear, which was willing to listen. *Don't listen to slander. There may be an element of truth in it, but slander destroys.* Totally crushed, Gordon took his family back to the hotel room. Sitting on the side of the bed, we again looked at each other and asked, "What do we do? Where do we go?" We were broke and broken, penniless and with nowhere to go. We were up against a stone wall so high we could not even see the top, much less see over on the other side. But God! A knock came on the door. It was Joann.

Gordon was very much beloved by the employees at Frank's car dealership. They were all heartbroken and in much depression. Joann came to him asking if he would stay and just walk through every day for a while, counseling and comforting them. In turn, she provided a house, food, and weekly allowance for us.

At that time we began to see a change in Corrie, our oldest. Up until this time, she was a very tenderhearted child. She wasn't a fighter and had a very hard time protecting herself from the constant bullying from kids at school and her "best friend", the girl next door in Spearfish.

Being a beautiful girl and the boys being attracted to her, the jealous girls were merciless to her to the point of throwing eggs at her at the football game. Finally, after meeting with the principal, she agreed to bring the girls into the office with Corrie. We went into intercession before the Father. The first thing out of Corrie's mouth was, "If I have done something to anger you, please tell me. What have I done? I am so sorry!" Immediately, the girls began to cry. They had no excuse or reason for their actions. They all became apologetic; the principal was overwhelmed by Corrie's humility. *Children can show us the way to reconciliation.* This was the beginning of our troubles with our older girls.

.

GORDON'S STORY

Our daughter, Heidi, decided to stay in Minnesota while the rest of family went on to Florida. I decided to get a job outside of the ministry and take time for our family to heal. We had very little money. I was looking for work and but was not able to find any. The Lord spoke to me, telling me to go to a men's prayer breakfast.

It was there that I sat down beside a man who turned to me and said, "Would you like to work for me?" He was a doctor who had a walk-in clinic. I became the person who checked in the patients. After work one Friday night the doctor and I were riding home when we got into a car accident. Someone ran us off the road into oncoming traffic. The car was totaled and I injured the heel of my right foot and needed crutches.

We were living in someone's house until we could get enough money to rent our own place. We were given three weeks to find a place. It was a bleak situation. We had no money. I was injured and could not work and we had three weeks before I needed to find another home. On Saturday I sat in the house feeling low and discouraged. On Sunday we went to church and went to a healing room with no faith and feeling very disheartened. A young man who was trained in Charles and Francis Hunter's ministry prayed for me.

I was so discouraged and had no faith. I thought I was finished. I let this guy go through the entire Hunter's prayer stuff. After he prayed for me, he said, "Do what you couldn't do before." I began to stamp my right foot and there was no more pain. Then I started jumping and praising God. God had healed me even when I was discouraged, upset, and hopeless. The faith of that young man brought healing to me. Thank you, Jesus.

On Tuesday, I went back to work. Along with working for the doctor, I also had a job at a Christian radio station and a security job. Unfortunately working all of those jobs still didn't meet the needs of our family but God provided. Many times people came up to me and blessed me with love gifts. I thank God for all of those generous and obedient people who have blessed us throughout the years.

Ramona made me promise not to put my name in for a church unless a church contacted us. It was a hard request but I said yes to it. During this time when there was a church service, day or night, I was there, praying, pressing in, and believing. It was not easy. God was killing the flesh and teaching me how to trust Him for total provision. The money I was making was not enough to cover our expenses but we paid our tithe and gave offerings and God made up the difference.

Many times I went from one job to the next just to take care of my family. At the church I was attending, they put me on the prophetic team. We would give the word of the Lord to people and in just days it would come to pass.

Those instant answers from God were difficult because nothing was happening for me. "Lord, how about me?" I would think.

For months, people would come up to me and say, "I got my job (or my house, car etc.), just like you said."

Then my car broke down and I did not have enough money to fix it. One day as I walked home from work, one of the men from the church saw me, stopped me, and said, "Why are you walking?" My reply was that my car had broken down. He took me to his garage and said, "Use my brand new car until you get yours fixed."

CHAPTER 24

GORDON'S STORY

Another day I received a call from a church in Alabama that wanted me to candidate for the church pastorate. I was getting an itch to pastor again after a year out of pastoring. When I sat down with the leaders, I told them about my ministry, including my deliverance and prophetic ministries, and that people of color would be welcome to come to the church. They said they had no problem with it at all.

The church offered me $1,500 a year to further my education for which I was very grateful. I made plans to attend a prophetic teaching school at Christian International in Florida. The school was for ten days, Monday through Friday. I was so sick the day I was to leave that I could not even carry my briefcase. They only have the teaching once a year so if I did not go this time, I would be one year behind in my journey.

In just two days, however, I was fine, and I never have been that sick again. I learned that I need to rebuke the devil and push through when he attacks. When I returned to the church after two weeks, one of the ladies of the church said, "You have changed so much. We don't see *you* we just see Jesus."

GORDON'S STORY

W e met this evangelist and I invited him to our church. He had a young musician traveling with him. The moment I saw this young musician, I knew that Corrie would marry him. I said nothing to anyone but, sure enough, they got married.

Later, he became our praise and worship leader. That was a challenge because the church members did not like his style. They thought it was too loud and that he sang too long. However when visitors came they all loved his music. *We were dealing with religious spirits again.* We were bringing in the new move of the Holy Spirit and the church was rejecting it. Soon the leadership asked me to release my son-in-law. That was such a difficult thing for me to have to do. Now we did not have a worship leader. The board asked who we were going to get now. My suggestion to them was to put an ad in the paper. I said it as a joke but that is exactly what they did.

The phone rang and the caller asked if we had found a worship leader yet and I said no. I told her to send her resume. They hired her; what a mess that was. While sitting on the platform one Sunday, I prayed, "Oh God, get me out of here." The next week, the leadership from the denomination came to speak to me because people in the church were not happy with me. I shared with them that there was a new move of the Holy Spirit coming and I was trying to get the church ready.

He said to me, "What about this prophetic thing?" I tried to explain it to him but he thought there were only Old Testament prophets. He didn't believe in the five-fold ministry.

"So Christ Himself gave the apostles, the prophets, the evangelists, the pastors and teachers, to equip His people for works of service, so that the body of Christ may be built up." Ephesians 4:11-12 NIV

They told me I no longer fit in the denomination and I needed to stop this "prophecy stuff". Then he said, "If the Holy Spirit goes this way and my denomination goes another, I will follow my denomination." Of course I resigned the church.

How can one keep preaching during the good times as well as the lean times? The key is that you realize that you are ministering unto the Lord not people. People will disappoint you. The Lord will not so keep a sweet humble spirit. Learn how to deal with rejection through forgiving and blessing those who reject you.

From there we tried to start another church about twenty miles away. It was tough going and the church never got off the ground.

We had to move from a very nice home to a 700-square-foot home. A dear sister let us stay there rent-free. We had to take out three pickup loads of trash and the walls were so dirty we could not paint them until we used a special cleaning solution on them first. We could hear rats in the walls. I got two cats and that took care of the problem. This was a very difficult time for us. During the next three years I never had a consistent pay check.

The Lord instructed me to take a bank deposit slip, fill it out for $10,000, and sing over it every day. My song was "I Am Going to Take You to the Bank" and for three years that is what I did. Sometimes I sang with great faith and other days I sang by faith.

One day a prophetess gave me a word that "money cometh" and each time she put her hand on my chest I felt something land on my chest. I told her, "Do that again!"

Shortly after that I got an invitation to preach at a prophetic conference in Florida. At that meeting, I met a man who two weeks later sent me $51,000 – five times more than what I was asking for. That gift gave us a fresh start in the ministry. All our bills were paid; we got two cars and new furniture and we moved into new rental in Prescott Valley, Arizona. I had $5,000 in savings, and we were rejoicing in the Lord.

Then, God spoke and said, "Give the $5,000 to help build the church in Prescott Valley."

My response was, "Father, I am saving money for a down payment on my house."

God said, "You take care of my house, and I will take care of your house." I obeyed and within six months, a man gave me $12,000 towards a new house. His son, who was a banker, helped us get the rest. Ramona had fun designing the house and building it.

Next we started a church in a warehouse in Prescott Valley. On Friday nights we had the School of the Holy Spirit where we raised up teams to prophesy. On Sundays and Wednesdays we had services as well. From there, I went into traveling full time as a prophetic evangelist. We stayed in motels and in people's homes. Whenever a family would put us up it turned into a special ministry time. Essentially we got to minister around the table as well as behind the pulpit. Since I had to start from zero again, the Lord used a brother to help me get three weeks of meetings scheduled which got me going.

GORDON'S STORY

I go wherever God opens the door and God has opened many doors…including preaching in a boxing arena in Mexicali, Mexico.

I frequently travel in Mexico, and I have preached in every Central American country, as well as Colombia, Chile, Germany, Nicaragua, and Canada. Wherever I go, God moves through signs, wonders, healings, miracles, and prophetic words. People get saved and baptized with the Holy Spirit. It amazes me!

While I was in Mexico once, I told a man who I had never met that within six months he would be pastoring. He now has a church of four hundred people.

One day, I received a call from a lady who said, "My doctor says the baby inside me is dead." They wanted to take the baby out that day, but she refused. We went to pray for her and rebuked death and released life on Monday. On Wednesday she went back to doctor. He checked her again and heard a heartbeat. Jesus brought the baby back to life.

Another anointing God has given me is to pray for barren women to have a child. Praise reports are constantly sent to us. I would say we have heard from well over 150 women, so many we have lost count.

During a meeting in California a lady came forward for healing in her back. I did not know she had steel rods in her back. As we prayed she began to jump up and down and bend over. The Lord healed her so she could use her back normally. For five years she had not been able to do that. Since that time, I have prayed for hundreds of people with back pain, and they have been healed.

I received this testimony for a couple who attended one of our meetings. *"My daughter was diagnosed with leukemia when she was only six months old. While she was being treated, the Lord sent you to the church we attended in Bakersfield, CA. We decided to come to hear you but we had to sit on the very last row because our daughter couldn't be around people. You called us to the front and declared, 'Life, Life, Life over death!' You cast out the spirit of death from our princess. About a year later, she was healed! On December 11, 2013 our daughter turned seven years old. She is cancer free. We are forever grateful for your life and our daughter's healing."*

In a meeting in Chula Vista, California, I called a man out of the audience, and I told him, "I see furniture," and the crowd gasped.

This man had just come from work where he sold furniture. At that point the Lord had his full attention. The Holy Spirit spoke and said that God was going to change his housing situation. They were living in a small home. Also the Spirit told him that there was going to be a meeting with his father. The next day he met with his father. An arrangement was made and he moved his wife and daughter to a $700,000 home.

Another time in Chula Vista, I said to a man, "You will pastor a church in six months," and that came to pass too. On another occasion, I went to a Mexican-American church. Most of the congregation had been delivered out a life of drugs and crime. The pastor gave me a check for $20,000. I was stunned. They only had about seventy people. He told me that one of the ladies was so touched that I love Mexican people that she wanted to give it to me.

I was in my office in South Dakota when the phone rang. "Pastor, I am in the hospital with a frozen foot," the man said. He had gotten caught for three days in a snow storm in below-zero weather. It was 10 AM and his foot was frozen and doctor said, "At 3 PM, I am coming to cut it off." We laid hands on the man's foot, and, at 3 PM, the doctor looked at it. It was turning pink and they did not remove his foot. Praise Jesus!

The Lord told me to tell a Latin American lady, "Hear the Word of the Lord: you will meet your husband in six months and he doesn't know Spanish, so you better learn English." At the time this lady was living with her children in a one-room apartment with a bath. Six months later she knew English, met her husband and they were married. God's blessing is upon them and now they live in a large house with a swimming pool.

I said to another man, "David, you will own your own ranch and have cattle and horses." He looked at me and said, "Thanks for the word; I would like to believe you." Three years later, he invited me to his ranch to brand his cattle. There had been some struggles along the way but he saw it through and hung onto his word from the Lord.

One day, I was helping some friends move into their new million dollar home. They were so excited. I turned to the lady of the house and said to her, "Enjoy this house for five years because you will sell it to a buyer for cash."

She said, "Pastor, I know you are a prophet, but I hope you are wrong." Five years later almost to the day, they sold their house for cash.

CHAPTER 27

GORDON'S STORY

I heard a great message by another evangelist entitled "Surely Goodness and Mercy Will Follow Me All the Days of My Life". It brought the house down when this evangelist shared it. He chose two guys out of the audience and instructed them to follow him around the church. He described different phases of life: sickness, pain, poverty, etc. When the preacher would run the two guys would also run.

The teaching went over so well that I decided to do it at a church in South Dakota. There was only one problem. One of the guys I had chosen for the demonstration was lagging behind and gasping for air. I kept yelling at him to go faster and faster. Later I discovered that he had recently undergone heart surgery! No surprise that the church never wanted me back. Needless to say, the next time I did that sermon, I first interviewed the two guys I chose to make sure they would survive.

"But those who trust in the LORD will find new strength. They will soar high on wings like eagles. They will run and not grow weary. They will walk and not faint." Isaiah 40: 31 NLT

ADVICE TO NEW MINISTERS

In my years of ministry, I have met some Christians that were fruitless, nasty, mean rascals. The ironic thing is that they praise Jesus, read the Bible, and speak in tongues, but they are just downright mean. The big problem seems to be controlling their tongue. Some Christians pride themselves in not smoking, drinking, chewing tobacco, or gambling, and on goes the self-righteous list. But they gossip.

My biggest disappointment in life has been the verbal attacks we have taken from other Christians. The lack of respect for ministers and their families is very sad. Many pastors' kids are not in church today because of how they saw their parents treated. That is why all of us must keep our eyes upon Jesus. There are many people who need to repent and ask forgiveness from their former pastors and their families. In one church I actually told the congregation, "This church is quarantined until you all get right; no one goes out, no one comes in."

The Lord told me one day, "I love the sinner too much to send them to a sick church." Many churches do not realize that they are sick and when you tell them, they get angry and want to kick you out. They do this by not paying their tithe. They starve you out.

If you think the ministry is a piece of cake, wake up. You have been drafted into a battlefield and you need to learn that you are more than a conqueror. In my time of pastoring, I have been asked to leave three churches. This record does not look good on a resume. Two out of the three churches do not exist today. Does that make me happy? No! We worked hard in those places. Two of the churches asked me to leave over the new worship style and the prophetic ministry. The good news is that there are more good sheep than bad.

Through the years, thousands of people have prayed for us and given to our ministry. The $5, $10, $20, $50, and $100 offerings are the backbone of our ministry budget. The Lord has also blessed us with a $51,000 and $100,000 offering in the last few years. If you are generous in the Kingdom of God you will be blessed. Our whole life has been a life of faith.

I have preached in churches, hotels, motels, tents, brush arbors, hair salons, barns, and houses. Wherever God opened a door, I went. I never demanded a certain amount of money to come and preach. God has been my source and has given me many surprises along this journey. For example numerous times my car stopped running, we would pray, and then it would start up again.

One day I will be a millionaire. Since 1970, I have confessed that I would be a millionaire. We have written out a deposit slip for ten million dollars, which I have in my possession. One day I will deposit millions in my account to further promote the Gospel.

CHAPTER 29

GORDON AND RAMONA

In our golden years, Ramona and I want to encourage, bless and send. We hope to have a place of refuge in Arizona and Wyoming with a ranch like setting. It will be a place where pastors and leaders can come and to be refreshed and blessed. They will be able to come with nothing and leave with much.

We also want to have a Holy Spirit Fire Training Camp for young people. We hope to purchase two buses that will sleep and house twelve girls in one bus and twelve boys in the other, with room for supervisors in each bus. We want to go into a city to hold meetings to assist the local church that has a vision for the lost and to disciple the new converts.

We plan to spend May through September in South Dakota, North Dakota, Wisconsin, and Montana. October through November we will have crusades in Latin America. In December we will take a break. Then, in January through April, we will be in California, Arizona, and Mexico.

We believe in the Joseph Generation: seven years of plenty and then seven years of drought. The church must be prepared to minister to the people and to take every opportunity to share Jesus with the people.

The bottom line is that we want to encourage young ministries and help them avoid the pitfalls of ministry life. My vision is to have young people come into my office and share their vision with me. I want to help them with their vision spiritually as well as financially. I want to build a relationship with these young ministers and to see their heart.

If I was not a preacher, I would have asked God to make me a wealthy business person so I could bless pastors, evangelists, teachers, prophets, apostles, widows, and orphans. In our lowest times financially, we always paid our tithe and gave our offerings. When God speaks to you to sow an offering, get ready to receive a blessing.

CHAPTER 30

IN CONCLUSION

In my walk with God, I have learned to love Him, trust Him, and serve Him. God has been good to me; He gave me Ramona and four wonderful daughters whom I love and who love me. I am truly blessed. – The German Shepherd

ABOUT THE AUTHORS:

Gordon Hofer, The German Shepherd, and Ramona Bunch Hofer, Honey Bunch, have been in ministry for over 40 years. Gordon has pastored, traveled as an evangelist in the Midwest during the '70s, built churches, had radio and TV programs, and preached internationally.

They have four married daughters and eleven grandchildren. They currently make their home in Prescott Valley, AZ.

Healing the Heartache of the Nations

Gordon.Hofer@yahoo.com